Éric Cartier, who was educated at Montreal University, is a journalist and translator. His early interest in classical and Chinese astrology was encouraged by his parents, they being of gypsy origin. He now holds frequent astrological surgeries in Montreal, his clients including several prominent politicians and artists. A Virgo with a Cancerian ascendant, he owns a large stationwagon and a gadget-filled hatchback, and has several children.

Louis T. Stanley was born under Capricorn. For many years he was Chairman and joint Managing Director (with Jean Stanley) of British Racing Motors. His other official posts include Director-General of the International Grand Prix Medical Service, Honorary Secretary and Treasurer of the Grand Prix Drivers' Association, Chairman of the Siffert Council and Trustee of the Jim Clark Foundation. He is much respected in motor-racing circles for his forthright views and the fearlessness with which he expresses them. He is the author of sixty-five books, of which the most recent, *Public Masks and Private Faces,* is published by Quartet. He lives in Trumpington, near Cambridge.

STAR CARS

ÉRIC CARTIER

STAR CARS

with an introduction and commentary by LOUIS T. STANLEY

illustrated by Jacques Lamontagne
translated by Lucinda Marchessini

Quartet Books
London   New York

First published by Quartet Books Limited 1986
A member of the Namara Group
27/29 Goodge Street, London WIP IFD

British Library Cataloguing in Publication Data

Cartier, Éric
  Star Cars
  1. Automobiles — Purchasing
  2. Astrology
  I. Title
  133.5'86292222   TL162

  ISBN 0-7043-0030-3

Typeset by Reprotype Ltd, Peterborough.
Printed and bound in Great Britain by
Nene Litho and Woolnough Bookbinding,
both of Wellingborough, Northants

CONTENTS

INTRODUCTION

Over the centuries, astrologers have read the signs of the zodiac, speculated on the influence of the sun, moon and planets, and analysed their effect upon the character, outlook and life of man.

In the 1950s a French statistician called Michel Gauquelin made a study which began as a cynical attempt to discredit the theory that the signs under which people are born can predetermine their way of life and choice of work. Gauquelin's debunking scheme had to be drastically revised when the survey surprisingly confirmed the theory. Examination of some 30,000 cases indicated that a significant percentage had been influenced in their choice of profession by their star-sign. The survey was extended to other European countries and the trend was again confirmed. Sceptics remained doubtful, but conceded that there was room for further research.

In the meantime Éric Cartier has indulged in a light-hearted incursion into the subject with a fanciful attempt to visualize how zodiac forces might affect one's ideal choice of car. Twelve imaginary cars are presented, one under each of the star-signs; I have matched each one with designers and men known for their involvement in cars, comparing their personalities, characteristics and tastes with those listed by Cartier.

I am inclined to think that Cartier would have had much in common with Heath Robinson, who would have revelled in such a project. Robinson was adept at producing humorous drawings of jerry-built cars constructed in a highly tortuous fashion for completely absurd purposes, fantasies which added a phrase to the language: a 'Heath Robinson' contraption conjures up an ingeniously impractical piece of apparatus, designed to carry out some simple task in the most complicated way, ideal for zodiac doodlings.

Looking for further inspiration, Cartier might have turned to fiction writers. Scott Fitzgerald described the automobile as an instrument of pleasure, of envy, and, in *The Great Gatsby,* of death, while the car in *The Diamond as Big as the Ritz* is a dream-vehicle worthy of any of Cartier's zodiacal creations. Aldous Huxley went further: in *Brave New World* he predicted that Ford would replace God. In so-called sculptural art, metal-junked cars often provide the basic material for exhibits, like the one in the New York Museum of Modern Art, while Saul Steinberg's drawings transform cars into weird baroque images against unreal backgrounds. On the other hand, Cartier might have played safe and looked for inspiration to the bourgeois respectability of suburbia and the insincerity of the stockbroker belt, as pictured in the world of John Betjeman and Miss Joan Hunter Dunn.

Before nominating the real-life designers and cars to parallel Cartier's astrological fantasies, it is pertinent to recall the basic principles of car design. A dream-car eludes a word or phrase, but takes shape in a visual image sustained in the mind. It is a visual rather than an aural chord, complicated by the fact that man is enamoured of it. No other inanimate object has produced such a close relationship; it has become an expression of man's personality. Psychiatrists say they know all about this: through his car man realizes his urge for freedom, for superiority and virility; it is a symbol of sexual prowess underlined by the use of phallic symbols in advertisements for cars and petrol.

It has been said that no man admits to doing two things badly – driving and making love. One well-known racing driver is fond of quoting this cliché. When I asked his long-standing female companion how he shaped in both departments, she replied that while he could drive well enough, his record of mechanical failures in the second department was nothing to boast about. I checked his zodiac sign with the Cartier formula and was not surprised.

Louis T. Stanley

AQUARIUS
21 JANUARY–19 FEBRUARY

According to many astrologists the world is heading towards the golden age of Aquarius, which will regenerate the whole human race. Hippies have been harping on this theme since 1968. It found expression in the famous song 'Aquarius', from the rock opera *Hair*.

People born under Aquarius have all-encompassing ideas. They are renowned for logical thinking. They love everybody, and their attitude to the world is very much a case of live and let live. They do not dominate others, and rarely pass judgement, even on those who are hostile towards them. Nor do they try to convert people to their way of thinking.

Aquarians consider justice and liberty to be fundamental human rights. Their concern for harmony between every race and creed is born of genuine conviction. Many lawyers are Aquarians, and this is attributed to their acute sense of right and wrong.

As parents, Aquarians are not nearly so strict as Capricorns. They are not weak, but in their anxiety to avoid being authoritarian they are sometimes a little too conciliatory. Their great virtue is that they treat their children as adults. They will always ask their point of view, for example, in the hope of persuading their children to become as fair and open-minded as they are.

Rarely do Aquarians become leaders. People say that this is because they lack assertiveness. It is rather a pity because, although they are less ambitious than Capricorns, Aquarians never abuse power and show themselves in every respect as capable as leaders, on the few occasions when they are given the opportunity.

If you have a problem which requires systematic thought, the chances are that an Aquarian will be able to solve it for you. When he has done so, however, he will give you the impression that you have solved it yourself.

Aquarians are very creative. Aware of their talent, they are generally confident in themselves and do not need to show aggression, which is a sure sign of self-doubt. They can, however, be rather dreamy and often they do not concentrate properly. Routines are repellent to them and unless (as is often the case) they are passionate about the job in hand, they may neglect to finish it.

The Aquarian loves to be inspired by new ideas, but he is less good at putting them into practice. He enjoys a philosophical argument, but will back down if it becomes heated. He is a poor combatant, except on paper, where he shows a natural feeling for words. He likes to fiddle about with computers.

Physique
Substantial build, languid movements, intelligent features, healthy complexion and, in most cases, fair hair.

Planetary Influence
Uranus — characterized by alternating good luck and misfortune.

Famous Aquarians
Modern figures: Franklin D. Roosevelt, Paul Newman, Mia Farrow.
Historical figures: Galileo, Mozart, Charles Dickens.

The Aquarian Car

This vehicle exists only in the fantasies of designers. By definition, the Aquarian car is streets ahead of the latest model on the market. When, in the fifties, General Motors proposed a joy-stick instead of a steering-wheel, they were only beginning to catch up with Aquarian thought. Similarly, Aquarians anticipated the turbo engine which converts alternative fuels to petrol, designed by Chrysler in the sixties. (This model was never put on the market.)

Nowadays the Aquarian dreams of a teardrop-shaped cockpit and unstressed glass-fibre body panels. The colour may be bright red or white. The front wheel spats, which remain static in their hub fixings, are ducted to extract cooling air from the brakes. The wheels themselves are optional, since the vehicle levitates like a hovercraft over road, sand and sea. The engine is a supercharged hydrogen turbo with an acceleration of 0-80 mph in 3.2 seconds.

Inside the cabin all electronics, including the instrumentation, air-conditioning and satellite navigation gear, are contained in a central module which extends as far as the front air intake, at bumper level. The car has a highly developed sixth sense and in times of danger will rush of its own accord to the aid of its owner.

Sadly, quite apart from the fact that this car has not yet been invented, Aquarians are unlikely to be able to afford it. This is because they are generally employed in poorly paid, creative professions. Aquarians who do have money to splash about, however, usually settle for the most technically advanced car at present available, such as a Gregory, Adsel, Citroën SM or Facel Vega. Many of them invested in the Tucker and de Lorean, the first of which never saw the light of day, the second of which saw it but never recovered from the shock. Moreover, because of the Aquarian's obsession with sophisticated fittings, it is difficult for him to get his car repaired locally, and almost impossible for him to sell it once it has lost its novelty, which of course happens very quickly. Car-ownership is therefore an extremely expensive and complicated business for Aquarians, but this does not worry them. Driving, they say, should be adventurous and fun, and they have little patience with people who would persuade them otherwise.

1 Electronic anti-theft locking system
2 Supercharged hydrogen turbo
3 Unstressed glass-fibre panels
4 Teardrop cockpit
5 Joy-stick
6 Instrumentation contained in central module
7 Front wheel spats
8 Air cushion

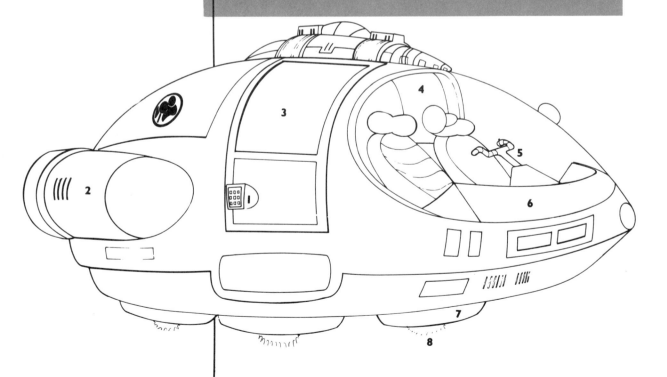

Fact or Fiction?

I am sorry for any Aquarian who resembles the Cartier blueprint; he sounds like a hippie nut-case. Continually plugging themes of justice and liberty, he seems to believe that love is the solution to every problem. There is nothing aggressive, competitive or assertive about him; he is just a wet.

Among genuine Aquarians, I can think of Jody Scheckter, a brilliant driver of fast machinery and a good tester; Bobby Unser, the irrepressible American and winner of the Indianapolis 500 on several occasions; John Surtees, who always knows all the answers; Jack Brabham, the laconic, unflappable Australian never beaten by a car; and most of all that Aquarian *par excellence*, Graham Hill, who for seven years was at the wheel of our BRM, in which he won ten of his fourteen Grand Prix and the Formula One World Championship. Graham had an immense capacity to enjoy life. At times he could be notoriously tactless. I once told him that he didn't know the difference between tongue-in-cheek and foot-in-mouth. His face could be immovably serene, but however grimly he pursed his lips, fiercely twitched his moustache and knitted his eyebrows, he could never assume the lineament of total displeasure. He lacked the tragic mask. During a crisis, and we had our share, his face would relax and assume a self-conscious, almost boyish grin. He was motor-racing's finest ambassador. If all Aquarians were like him, life would be much pleasanter.

My Aquarian designer would be the Austrian, Dr Porsche, who created not one famous car but many. He began with Lohner in Austria, changed to Austro-Daimler in 1905, and was responsible for the superb 'Prince Henry' models. The next change was Daimler in Stuttgart. In 1928 he returned to Austria to set up his own design offices from which came the Beetle and the first of the mid-engined Auto Union racing cars. After the Second World War he advised Renault in 1945 on their new small car, but the war years took a toll on his health. He died in 1951, leaving his son Ferry to carry on the Porsche tradition.

PISCES
20 FEBRUARY-21 MARCH

PISCES
20 FEBRUARY-21 MARCH

Pisces is the most idealistic sign in the zodiac. People born under the sign of the fish are highly nonconformist. Many of them are artists, poets and philosophers. They dislike competition, and have a horror of being in the limelight. They are sometimes rather elusive, and slip with consummate ease through nets in which other creatures become hopelessly enmeshed.

It would be wrong to say that Pisceans have no ambition, but it is not easily apparent. Because they are so reflective they are often prey to bouts of depression. Here the familiar evils of lethargy, drugs and alcohol come into play. Nevertheless, Pisceans often excel in art and literature. But the road to success is long and arduous and there are likely to be several accidents on the way.

Their elusiveness apart, Pisceans are very good-natured and have a curious tendency to trust other people too readily. This often makes them dupes.

Imagination and a highly developed sense of beauty are Piscean characteristics. They enjoy solitude and daydream perpetually. Many of them dabble in mysticism. They are at their best in partnership with people of a more dynamic nature, such as Arians, who will not let them waste their talents. A typically Piscean thing to do would be to set up a canvas with the intention of painting a masterpiece, and then spend all day deciding which brush to use.

Pisceans lead interesting lives because they refuse to conform. They do more or less what they want to do, but they would do still more if only they could make up their minds. They view conventional notions of success with suspicion and are as open to new ideas as Aquarians. They make good teachers and devoted friends. Their patience is legendary.

Physique
Smallish stature, often pale complexion, well-proportioned hands and feet, graceful and expressive movements.

Planetary Influences
Neptune — charaterized by the arts, poetry and mysticism.

Famous Pisceans
Modern figures: Auguste Renoir, Albert Einstein, Enrico Caruso, John Steinbeck, Elizabeth Taylor, Rudolf Nureyev. Historical figures: Michaelangelo, George Washington, Frédéric Chopin.

The Piscean Car

Like the Capricorn, the Piscean is not a car enthusiast. He will not own an old banger, which would offend him aesthetically, but he takes no interest in special big-bore pistons or gas-flowed high-compression cylinder-heads. He is much keener on boats. The more closely a car resembles a boat the more likely a Piscean is to admire it. The shark-like 1948 Studebaker and gleaming 1950 Kaiser were much esteemed by Pisceans.

Psychologists often talk of the subconscious desire to go back to the womb. Pisceans are particularly prone to this desire. Some atrologers go so far as to say that to the Piscean, the car represents a sort of metaphorical womb. Certainly, he regards it as a refuge in which he can hide from the bewildering complexities of the world outside.

The ideal Piscean car resembles a long, pale-blue boat gliding gracefully through the city traffic. In its stately silence it evokes the mysterious depths of the kingdom of Neptune. The windows are tinted green and bubbles float prettily from the exhaust pipe.

Next to beauty, comfort is the Piscean's chief concern. He insists on dynamic tracking suspension. The seats are of blue and grey brushed velvet and the air-conditioning is intended less to cool the car than to exclude external noise. The Piscean enjoys a chat and has a CB radio for this purpose, but he is at his happiest listening to Mozart concertos on the 25-watt four-speaker stereo system.

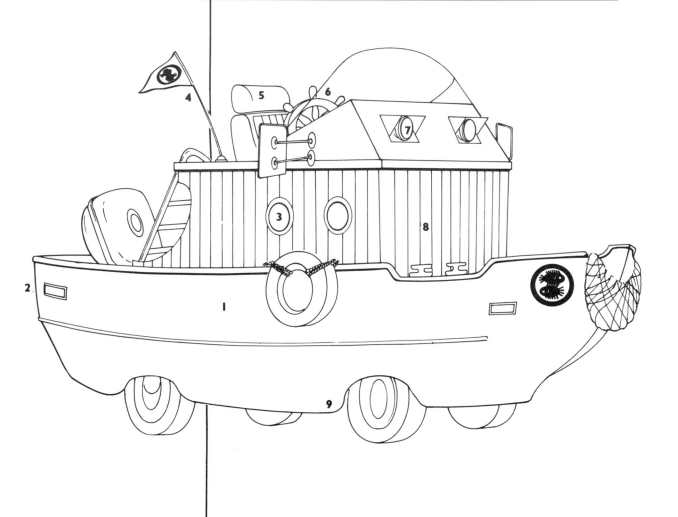

1 Glass-fibre hull
2 Bubble exhaust system
3 Portholes tinted green
4 CB radio
5 Skipper's blue and grey brushed-velvet seat
6 Helm
7 Searchlights
8 Cabin
9 Dynamic tracking suspension

Fact or Fiction?

I have to take issue with Cartier here. There have been several notable Pisceans in the motor industry and none of them would have lasted long if, as Cartier suggests, they regarded their cars as metaphorical wombs and were prey to depression and lethargy. It would be ridiculous to attribute such characteristics to Alain Prost, Brian Redman, Niki Lauda, Peter Gethin and, that rare individual, Malcolm Campbell.

When it comes to the Piscean designer, none could compete with Enzo Ferrari, a man of mercurial moods, of sudden generosity and equally sudden temper, at times unemotional; it never does to underestimate his capability or determination to get his own way. The Commendatore is a law unto himself. I have found him a formidable opponent for many years, persistant, at times unscrupulous, and not always ethical, but single-minded in endeavour. The name of Ferrari is respected, not only in Italy, but throughout the automobile world, as that of the autocratic doyen of motor-racing.

ARIES
22 MARCH–20 APRIL

People born under the sign of the ram are full of courage, energy and ambition. At an early age they discover that their friends depend on them for advice and guidance. Consequently they develop into outstanding leaders. They love nothing more than a challenge. Blessed with initiative and extreme vitality, they long to get things changed. If you have a bold and radical scheme you should ask an Arian to take charge of it.

Sadly, there is a negative side to these qualities. Arians can be excessively aggressive. They have no sense of modesty and abhor taking orders from other people. This makes them notoriously difficult employees. The desire to command is so deeply rooted inside them that they are quick to rebel against authority, even when they lack the competence to criticize it. Talented Arians advance meteorically. Others merely offend with their constant carping and often find themselves out of a job.

No one is more stubborn than the Arian. He will only listen to advice when it corresponds to what he thinks already. Moreover, he says exactly what he means, regardless of the consequences. Timid people are often seriously upset by his tactless remarks. On the other hand, he is never malicious or deceptive. If an Arian has something unpleasant to say to you, he will say it, and that is the end of the matter. This is perhaps his greatest virtue.

Socially, Arians are enormous fun. They are constantly being asked to parties, and no one is better at turning a dullish evening into a wild night out. Unfortunately their tendency to over-indulge themselves has a bad effect on their health, of which they take not the slightest notice. Many Arians are completely burnt out by the age of forty.

Peaceful types dislike Arians. If, on the other hand, you want to live to the full and never get bored, the Arian is an excellent companion. But be careful. He is very quick to insist upon his own freedom, but much less good at allowing freedom to others. In romantic connections especially the Arian can be fiercely possessive.

Physique
Medium build, complexion and hair usually dark, thick eyebrows often meeting in the middle, well muscled and agile.

Planetary Influences
Mars and the Sun, characterized by enthusiasm, courage and determination. The Sun symbolizes power and honour.

Famous Aquarians
Modern figures: Charlie Chaplin, Arturo Toscanini, Tennessee Williams, Marlon Brando, Warren Beatty, Doris Day.
Historical figures: Charlemagne, Leonardo da Vinci, Johann Sebastian Bach.

The Arian Car

Aggression is the chief characteristic of the Arian car. Its owner loves to draw attention to himself and favours a fiery red bodywork and an enormous engine. He fondly remembers the days when the American V-8s dominated the highway, with their eight-litre cylinders and giant carburettors. Few things are more delightful to the Arian than to leap ahead when the lights go green, leaving the rest of the traffic in a blaze of exhaust fumes and burning rubber. He is always revving impatiently. Before fuel became so expensive he used to drive, in order of preference, the Jaguar V-12, the Camaro Z-28 and the 340 Demon Dodge.

Nowadays most Arians are obliged to settle for smaller models, but they still insist on speed. A smooth performance is less important than a powerful one. The engine is turbo-charged, the transmission reinforced and the shock-absorbers regulated. The suspension is raised and the wheels are alloy or magnesium.

If an Arian is overtaken on the road he regards it as a personal challenge. He will push his engine remorselessly to catch up again, often with scant regard to safety. Other motorists, even medallioned spivs in Italian sports cars, tend to avoid him. Yet there is no bitterness in the Arian's approach to driving; it is merely part of his competitive nature.

As a general rule Arians are not much interested in gadgets. Their principal demand is for a sense of power, and this is usually conveyed by chrome exhaust pipes or side-intakes ducted with a venturi tunnel to minimize drag. In America the brasher Arians have a habit of hanging a racoon's tail from the aerial. Their British counterparts draw attention to themselves by displaying their Christian names on the windscreen.

Arians are always rushing about and consequently favour four-wheel drive for a performance equally powerful over snow-capped mountains and wind-swept sand dunes. Their ideal car would be designed on the basis of three existing models: the turbocharged Volvo Beast, the 1948 Buick Roadmaster and the old Mustang Boss.

1 Turbo
2 Giant carburettor
3 Racoon's tail suspended from aerial
4 Rocket booster
5 Side intakes
6 Customized rear wheels
7 Regulated shock-absorbers
8 Iodized headlights

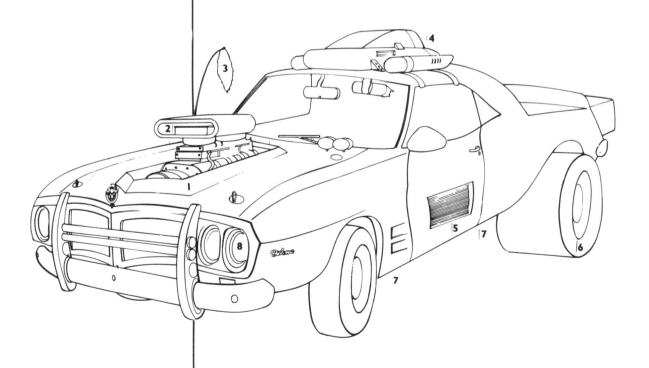

Fact or Fiction?

According to Cartier, Arians are noted for courage, energy and ambition. They love a challenge; possess immense initiative and vitality, but can be aggressively awkward. So far so good. Arians like Jean-Pierre Beltoise fit the bill admirably. At his best the little Frenchman is brilliant, in total control of himself and the car, as he demonstrated when winning the Monaco Grand Prix at the wheel of a BRM. Conditions were appalling with continuous torrential rain, but not once did he make a mistake. Carlos Reutemann was another in the same mould. The macho Argentinian used to show incredible consistency, particularly in the 1980 World Championship when he had a series of fifteen consecutive finishes, building up a seventeen-point lead in the 1981 title hunt, although he lost the championship to Piquet by one point. He reflected many Arian traits, rather like Riccardo Patrese and Didier Pironi.

It is only when we come to the Arian car that there are differences of opinion. The emphasis on speed is accurate, but few would approve the brash design. Instead I turn to the creative outpourings of a man born at Alwalton, near Peterborough, son of a flour miller, his mother the daughter of a farmer. The father died when the boy was ten, so Henry Royce had to earn his living as a newspaper boy, messenger boy, and then apprentice to the locomotive works at Peterborough. Shortage of money cut short his apprenticeship. He went to work in a Leeds tool factory, then became a tester with an electrical company, studied at night-school and eventually became chief electrical engineer. In 1884 he founded F.H. Royce and Company, manufacturing arc lamps, dynamos and electrical cranes in Manchester. His experience with an early motor car led him to design and make motor cars himself and in 1904 he produced his first ten-horse-power two-cylinder Royce car. Its silence, smoothness and flexibility were so remarkable that C. S. Rolls, who had a selling agency for cars in London, offered to buy the entire output of Royce cars and sell them as Rolls-Royce.

In 1906 the merger took place with Royce as engineer-in-chief and Rolls technical managing director. Between them they produced and marketed what is still not only the finest but the best-loved car in the world. It symbolizes dignity with no suggestion of gimmickry. The finished product confirms the legend on the front entrance of the works at Crewe: *Quiduis Recte Factum Quamvis Humile Praeslarem – Whatever rightly done, however humble, is noble.* Royce was the dominant partner. He had no intention of producing a wide range of models. He preferred to perfect one type of vehicle. By the end of 1906 the forty- to fifty-horse-power Silver Ghost was launched and remained the prototype until 1925 when the Phantom and Wraith appeared.

Perhaps the significant point is that an Arian had joined forces with a Gemini.

TAURUS
21 APRIL–20 MAY

TAURUS
21 APRIL–20 MAY

Taureans are calm, systematical, persevering and affectionate. They have the gentle strength of the bull and (except when provoked into rage) their movements are slow and deliberate. They are solid types who set themselves goals and do everything in their power to attain them.

When things go wrong it is comforting to have a Taurus at hand. He seldom panics or loses his sensible approach. Indeed, he rather relishes difficulties because he knows that in solving them he displays himself to best advantage.

The Taurus is not niggardly but hates to see money wasted. He dislikes frivolities. He is a good administrator and organizes himself well. He lives to the full without burning the candle at both ends.

In appearance the Taurus is generally sober, which often leads to the assumption that he is dull. In fact he has a rich sense of humour which some people find rather lacking in delicacy. It is true that he often jokes about bodily functions, but there is no real harm in it. He also often jokes about himself, which is an endearing characteristic and all too rare in other people.

Rare too is the Taurean sense of honesty. Along with his other qualities this guarantees success at work. Where the Taurus does not climb to the top of his profession he comes a very good second, and invariably enjoys the affection and respect of his colleagues.

Taureans make good parents and adore family life, at the risk of becoming too exclusively domestic. Their houses are always comfortable and liberally stocked with modern conveniences, as long as they are genuinely useful: silly gadgets offend their sense of purpose.

Never taunt a Taurus. He may seem placid enough, but if you provoke him he will suddenly erupt in rage. Like a hapless matador impaled on the horns of a bull, you may not live to regret your insolence.

Taureans make good judges because they are not hampered by prejudice and never come to a conclusion before they have the full facts. They are quick to overlook little faults, but sometimes expect to find too many of their own good qualities in other people.

Physique
Not very tall, broad-shouldered, deliberate movements, fairly dark hair and eyes, large eyes and mouth, solemn and melodious voice.

Planetary Influence
Venus – symbolizes love. Here more love of the family than erotic love.

Famous Taureans
Modern figures: Sigmund Freud, Adolf Hitler, Harry Truman, Queen Elizabeth II, Fred Astaire, Perry Como.
Historical figures: William Shakespeare, Brahms, Tchaikovsky.

The Taurean Car

Comfort is the Taurean's chief concern in driving. He loves to lounge about in a Rolls or, failing that, an old-fashioned American limousine such as the sixties' Lincoln Continental or even the pre-war La Salle. The poorer Taureans favour French cars, whose manufacturers place so much emphasis on ergonomics. This is the study of the relationship between your well-being and your environment. The French designers construct their cars around the human shape, and as a result even the cheaper models are famed for their comfort. The Citroën DS-21 is particularly impressive in this respect.

Speed is not important to the Taurus. To tell the truth he is rather afraid of it. This is one of the reasons why the Rolls suits him so well. It is a splendid, stately vehicle but hardly renowned for its acceleration. Indeed, its manufacturers are reluctant to tell you what its acceleration is.

Inside the Taurean's ideal car is a small bar with a fridge, a telephone, a thick sheepskin carpet, air-conditioning, a leather-bound steering-wheel, a walnut dashboard and an eight-speaker stereo system. The seats are covered in velvet and can adjust to a limitless number of positions.

Recently a television programme in the United States showed how an eccentric had converted his ancient Cadillac into what he described as 'the most comfortable car in the world'. It boasted a chemical lavatory, a washbasin, a colour television and a video. Needless to say the man was a Taurus.

The more conservative Taureans favour dark green, the less so bright green or orange. They all have rather refined natures (except, of course, for their dirty jokes) and generally prefer to be chauffeur-driven.

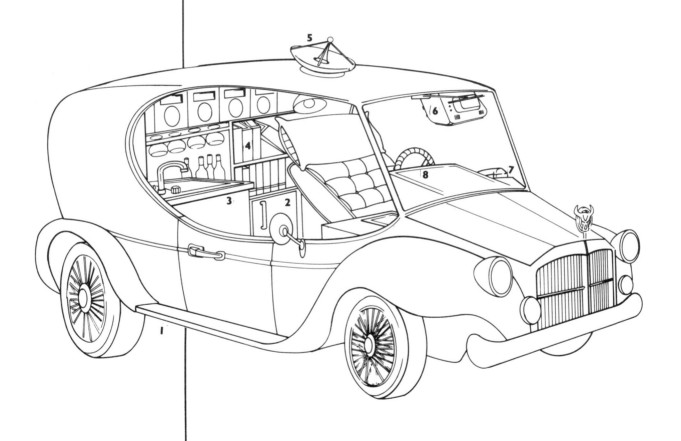

1 Regulated suspension
2 Refrigerator
3 Bar/sink
4 Library
5 Radar reflector
6 VDU linked to Dow Jones Stock Exchange
7 Telephone
8 Walnut dashboard

Fact or Fiction?

To my mind Colin Chapman was the ideal Taurean. Many of the characteristics described by Cartier applied to him, although he would have scorned the eccentricities of Cartier's ideal Taurean car, and to suggest that he was frightened of speed would be very wide of the mark: he was one of the world's outstanding designers of racing cars. His influence on British machinery was remarkable. The record book has the details, but fails to do justice to the extent of his achievements. He was dynamic, an unceasing worker, tireless in enthusiasm with a reputation as a perfectionist, though at times he did cut corners which upset purists. He had a flair for infecting others with the belief that miracles were not only possible, but expected. He could be ruthless, was withering when it came to incompetence, and he had the Taurean fiery temper. A shrewd businessman with the confidence and aplomb to tackle anyone, Colin was never impressed by public reputations. When he talked about his work, he did so directly with neither false modesty nor pretentiousness. Off the circuit, he was excellent company, a lively conversationalist. With strong personalities you tend to see the world through their eyes. Chapman was no exception. The future for him was one long challenge in a highly competitive area. Tragically, he died at the peak of his powers.

GEMINI
21 MAY–21 JUNE

Everybody knows that Geminis lead double lives. Very often they have two jobs at the same time. Invariably they have several different interests, which are sometimes contradictory. For example, it is not uncommon for a Gemini to be a keen angler and a member of the anti-bloodsports league. Their love-life is particularly complicated because they are always chasing two or more partners at once. Their moods change dramatically. They may be feverishly enthusiastic one moment, and hopelessly depressed the next.

Because Geminis are so mercurial it is difficult to assess their other characteristics. Generally, however, they are alert and talkative. Patience is not one of their virtues and they are often somewhat explosive. They will not tolerate people who are less intelligent than they are and they tend to snap at you if you have missed the point.

A curious thing about Geminis is that they age very well. Long after their contemporaries have lost their looks Geminis retain their youthful expression and sprightly demeanour. This often leads to jealousy.

At work, Geminis tend to take on far too much and leap from one project to another without completing either. Nevertheless, they have strong creative powers and are particularly good at selling things. They also adapt easily to new surroundings.

Geminis love modern gadgets and take to computers like ducks to water. They are great charmers and are famed for seducing people, both sexually and as eloquent salesmen, comedians, barristers and advertisers. They often get into trouble but seldom fail to get out of it.

Being married to a Gemini can be a harrowing experience. Their thirst for novelty exceeds their faithfulness. The divorce courts are full of errant Gemini wives and husbands.

Seldom is the Gemini punctual, but you forgive him for it because his company is so stimulating. His energy rivals that of the Arean. Sadly, it has the same effect on his health, which, for all his apparent vigour, is generally rather delicate.

Physique
Tall and slender, rapid movements, sometimes rather unco-ordinated, pale complexion, delicate features.

Planetary Influence
Mercury — symbolizes intellect.

Famous Geminis
Modern figures: John F. Kennedy, Marilyn Monroe, Bob Hope, Bob Dylan.
Historical figures: Socrates, Queen Victoria, Sir Arthur Conan Doyle.

The Gemini Car

Like his Mercurian partner Virgo, the Gemini loves the colour blue. But he is even fonder of two-tone cars. These were very prevalent in America in the fifties, and the majority of people who bought them were Geminis.

Their ideal car is dual in every respect. It has a double axle, double headlights, two spare wheels, two stereo systems, and a double engine (like that of the 2CV Citroën). There is a driver's seat and dashboard at each end, enabling the car to travel backwards and forwards with equal ease.

Pending the manufacture of such a vehicle, the Gemini often settles for owning two cars of a wholly different character. He might drive, for example, a sports car and a camping van, or a double-decker bus and a Fiat 400. It would amuse him to place one such vehicle inside the other, so that he could park the bus in a dual carriageway lay-by and make a brisk excursion down the local country lanes in his Fiat. Alternatively, he might attach a Lotus Mark 6 to the back of his camping van.

Less eccentric Geminis are still prone to driving sober-looking family saloons with mighty 4.2 litre engines inside them, a unitary chassis and an Audi rally Quattro-type automatic clutch. The younger Geminis are often keen on vintage cars, but once again they will equip them with powerful modern engines. The aim is to lull everybody into a false sense of security with their ancient appearance and then roar ahead of the rest of the traffic when the lights go green.

Geminis are natural chameleons and adore teasing people or taking them by surprise, but there is no malice in it. They enjoy driving every bit as much as Arians, but they do not enter into it with the same fierce spirit of competition. Their intention is simply to entertain.

1 Six coats of paint (i.e. twice the normal three)
2 Two engines with double camshaft and twin carburettors
3 Four foglights
4 Dual controls
5 Double headlamps concealed behind radiator grill
6 Twin tyres

Fact or Fiction?

Cartier says that Geminis lead double lives, make good salesmen, are generally talkative and adept at getting out of trouble. Those who are Geminis are at liberty to decide for themselves, but the probability is that they will match up. I can think of three. Innes Ireland is an extrovert character whose antics detracted from his racing ability, but he is always good value. Denny Hulme, the former world champion, is so dour that there must be another side to his life. Jackie Stewart would find a double life too restricting. He is certainly talkative, in fact there must be times when his patient wife, Helen, wishes he would catch tonsilitis.

Then there was Charles Stewart Rolls, son of Lord Llangattock. He had many Gemini touches. Wealthy, debonair, man-about-town, he founded the Royal Aero Club and was one of our pioneering aviators. He often tried to persuade his partner Royce to design an aero-engine, but Royce would let nothing interfere with his engineering until the First World War. Then he produced the 'Eagle' engine which had a significant role in the war, and followed it with the 'Falcon', 'Hawk', 'Condor' and 'Merlin' engines, the last one featuring in the Second World War. Rolls-Royce were also involved in the Schneider Cup competitions and won the trophy in 1929 and 1931, setting up a world speed record of 408 mph. Rolls' enthusiasm for flying had tragic consequences. In July 1910 his Wright aeroplane had a structural failure when flying over Bournemouth and crashed with fatal results.

CANCER
22 JUNE–23 JULY

Cancerians are grand sentimentalists. They demand the affection and approval of others. Unlike Arians or Leos, they are not at all ostentatious, but all the same they like their achievements to be noticed. Many of them are teachers, at which they excel, because winning the respect of the class is their first objective.

Nothing is more sacred to the Cancerian than family life, unless it is his friends. He feels threatened by the outside world and the smallest criticism can reduce him to misery. He often attempts to hide his vulnerability behind a rather brittle exterior, but it is easy to see through. He looks back upon his childhood as a sort of lost paradise, regardless of what it was actually like. If you see a Cancerian deep in thought he is probably dreaming of his mother.

Cancerians have an obsessive habit of collecting things. Their houses are invariably crammed with useless mementoes which help them to reconstruct the past. This gives them a sense of continuity and purpose in life.

If you upset a Cancerian he will never forget it. He weighs his own actions carefully, and is equally analytical of other people's. He judges himself very harshly, and often comes to the conclusion that he is completely useless. You have to work hard to convince him otherwise. In many ways Cancerians are admirable people, but there is no getting away from the fact that they tend to make mountains out of molehills and often bear grudges wholly out of proportion to the offence you have given them.

Silence, soft light and familiar surroundings are essential to the Cancerian's well-being. He hates noise. Darkness worries him and strangers put him on his guard. Anything remotely unpredictable is sure to upset him for weeks.

Cancerians love family outings and are always dragging their children off to the seaside or on camping trips. They take photographs relentlessly. Often they own little dinghies. They are likewise fond of gardening and cooking.

It is good fun to have a Cancerian parent, except for his excessive domesticity. He is a devoted teacher and an efficient employee, the sort of person who for all his self-doubt, has a stabilizing influence on others.

Physique
Average height, broad shoulders, long limbs, usually prominent chin, surprisingly big feet.

Planetary Influence
Moon — symbolizes emotion and desire.

Famous Cancerians
Modern figures: John D. Rockefeller, Ernest Hemingway, Ringo Starr, Arthur Ashe.
Historical figures: Julius Caesar, Henry VIII, Rembrandt, John Quincy Adams.

The Cancerian Car

The Cancerian father invariably owns a family saloon into which he bundles his eager fledgelings for picnics on Sundays. The size of the vehicle naturally depends on the size of the family. Many Cancerians convert school buses into campers. Those with four or fewer children drive minivans or stationwagons. Those who are as yet childless take their friends for fishing or shooting trips in four-wheel-drive Cherokee jeeps.

All these vehicles have roof-racks heaped with camping gear and hunting trophies, such as the stuffed head of a moose. At the back is a trailer whose contents vary with the season — surfing equipment, skis, racing bikes and bits of scenery from school theatre productions. There is also an ice-dispensing machine to appease querulous kiddies, and the windows are plastered with stickers proclaiming 'Traffic wardens are nice people — back in five minutes!'

The United States is a Cancerian country, with Gemini in the ascendant. Not surprisingly, the family car originated in America, and apart from a brief eclipse in the sixties, when it was considered rather unfashionable, it has always been America's most popular mode of transport. Nowadays one has to wait up to six months for a model in one's favourite colour, which for Cancerians, who are lunar creatures, is usually a metallic grey.

1 Luggage compartment containing ice-dispenser
2 Racing bikes
3 Skis
4 Television
5 Stuffed moose head
6 Jolly stickers
7 Seats for all the family
8 Detachable cabin with three wheels for short excursions

Fact or Fiction?

For types who according to their zodiac signs should be
hesitant and vulnerable to criticism, there are many
personalities in the automobile world who seem to have
done quite well. Names like John Cooper, whose
designing skill made such an impact in Formula One
motor-racing; Fangio, one of the world's finest racing
drivers; Patrick Tambay, who radiates gaiety with a
personality that makes an immediate appeal; and René
Arnoux, who comes nearest to showing Cancerian traits,
for, though he has enormous talent, at times he seems to
have inner doubts and mental deafness.

LEO
24 JULY–23 AUGUST

As you would expect, Leos are noble, proud and generous. They inspire confidence in other people, never bear grudges, and are tremendously ambitious. They are, however, a little too fond of showing off.

The Leo makes light of danger and adversity, convinced that he will be able to overcome them. In this respect he is usually right, but when he doesn't get what he wants he takes it very badly. He is so used to success that he cannot countenance failure, and being a dominant sort of person, he makes everybody feel as wretched about it as he does.

Leos are natural leaders and do not like people to tell them what to do. If you step on their toes they will make life extremely uncomfortable for you. Nevertheless they will do so openly and give you a fair chance to put your point of view. Leos are far too noble to resort to underhand methods, even when they could profit by them.

Generally speaking, women who dominate offices are Leos. They take an active role in all sorts of fields, from feminist agitation to organizing church fetes. Very often they are company directors; their forcefulness knows no bounds. This is not to say that they lack grace or charm. Indeed, they are highly attractive, but they will not let anyone take advantage of them. Dating a female Leo can be hard work, but it is usually worth it.

Ostentation is the Leo's biggest fault. However, he is aware of this and struggles to maintain the bold, straightforward approach to life which people so greatly admire in him. He is full of love for his family, but sometimes expects its members to be of similar temperament to himself. This makes him too demanding, and can lead to hard feelings.

Like Cancerians, Leos enjoy teaching but they are better at lecturing. They are apt to have well-defined theories which you should challenge with extreme caution. It is not that they dislike being contradicted — indeed if your point is valid and intelligent they welcome it — but they will not stand for woolly argument.

Physique
Well proportioned, impressive stature, large head, haughty expression.

Planetary Influence
The Sun — characterized by power, honour and decorum.

Famous Leos
Modern figures: Benito Mussolini, Jacqueline Kennedy-Onassis, Alfred Hitchcock, Fidel Castro.
Historical figure: Napoleon.

The Leo Car

When it comes to driving Leos tend to give in to their love of ostentation. Most of them prefer carriages to cars, and given the choice would opt for a gilded coach drawn by six horses, such as the Queen uses on state occasions. However they are not averse to the Rolls Corniche with fine leather cushions, or to the Silver Ghost with six windows and a chauffeur staring fixedly at the Winged Victory adorning the radiator cap.

Sadly, for all their vigour and ambition, Leos can seldom encompass such extravagance. Indeed many of them are forced to buzz about in decrepit VW Beetles. All the same they tend to decorate the bonnets with Rolls-Royce radiator grills – a popular craze in Canada recently. Even Leos with quite grand cars acquire all sorts of extras to make them grander, such as magnesium wheels and walnut dashboards.

Leos are governed by the sun and consequently adore the colour gold. In Texas they often drive Cadillacs with gold-plated bumpers and a pair of bull's horns embossed in brass on the bonnet. European Leos have a habit of painting their coats of arms on the doors of their Citroën CXs or Peugeot 604s.

The ambition to become President of the United States is extraordinarily common among Leos in America. This is partly because they covet the presidential bullet-proof limousine with its attendant host of bodyguards poised upon the running-boards. Pending their election they are content to drive a black Cadillac Ceville with an auburn leather interior, or a similarly upholstered Daimler or Mercedes. Some go so far as to cover their cars in lion-skins.

1 Gold-plated bumper
2 Loudspeakers playing military marches
3 Gold-plated radiator
4 Twelve-cylinder engine
5 Walnut dashboard
6 Hunting horns
7 Leather seats
8 Running-boards for bodyguards
9 Lion-shaped headlights

Fact or Fiction?

If the influence of Leo has had real effect on an automobile designer, I nominate a farmer's son who was born in 1863 under that sign. The lad, fascinated by the mechanism of clocks and watches, worked in a Detroit machine-shop at the age of sixteen, where he became interested in automobile design. In 1896 he produced a brakeless, reverseless, two-cylinder vehicle that, in spite of its appearance, actually worked. He ignored criticisms, managed to attract financial backing, and in 1908 produced one of the ugliest and most adaptable cars ever made, the Model T Ford, the creation of Henry Ford 1.

It was a 2.9-litre, four-cylinder engine cast in one piece with a detachable cylinder-head, in itself a revolutionary innovation. The narrow chassis was on transverse springs with a remarkable steering-lock. Other oddities included no hand gearshift or accelerator. The two speeds and reverse were controlled by three foot pedals. Small brakes on the rear wheels were dependent on a hand-lever. The customer, according to Ford, could have a choice of colour provided it was black. Its popularity was such that between 1917 and 1927 half the cars produced in the United States of America were Tin Lizzies. By 1924 mass-production techniques had lowered the selling price to 290 dollars.

The Leos described by Cartier are Walter Mittys with Rolls-Royce ideas and Ford pockets. As types they are petulant, spoilt, generous, over-demanding and resentful of authority. The suggested car reflects a James Bond mentality with Liberace tastes, a nightmare on wheels, and hardly likely to appeal to such Leos as Nelson Piquet, the quiet man of racing who keeps out of the limelight but has complete sympathy with his machinery; Patrick Depailler, the son of an architect who can handle anything on wheels; that pair of fastidious Leos, Raymond Mays and Louis Chiron, both sadly missed, outspoken critics of car design; but not so scathing as Sir William Lyons, a stylist for over fifty years and creator of the SS, SS-Jaguar, and the XJ-S. He would have made mincemeat of this vulgar concept.

VIRGO
24 AUGUST–23 SEPTEMBER

VIRGO
24 AUGUST–23 SEPTEMBER

Virgos are practical and intelligent. They usually have excellent memories. They are not very fond of manual work, but excel in writing and research. Many of them are journalists. They are extraordinarily good at assimilating complex information and presenting it simply.

The Virgo is of far quieter disposition than the Leo or Arian, and he does not often do full justice to his talents. Nevertheless he usually manages to climb quite high in his chosen field, and he has a knack of exercising a great deal of influence from the sidelines. Ambitious types tend to manipulate him to their own ends, reckoning that he is unlikely to pose any threat to their aspirations. The Virgo is well aware of this, but regards it with serene indifference.

Their high standards often make it difficult for Virgos to get on with other people. The problem is that they are hypercritical. When they do find friends it is usually among their fellow Mercurians, the Geminis. They are very perfectionist and, although this makes them able administrators, they have a horror of delegating.

The Virgo is more cerebral than emotional. He tends to bottle up his feelings, and as a result he can be insensitive to other people's. Nevertheless, he is normally well-intentioned, but because of his natural reticence one can easily overlook it. To make things worse, he is generally economical to the point of miserliness.

Oddly enough there have been a good many Virgo comedians, so one cannot say that they never rise above their timidity. Moreover, the older Virgos are far less shy. But as a general rule Virgos like to remain in the background, working diligently away in a quiet but relentless pursuit of knowledge.

Physique
Angular face, regular features, usually dark hair, average height and stature.

Planetary Influences
Mercury — symbolizes intellect and business sense.

Famous Virgos
Modern figures: Leo Tolstoy, Colette, Greta Garbo, Peter Sellers, Leonard Bernstein, Sophia Loren.
Historical figures: Alexander the Great, Queen Elizabeth I, Christopher Columbus, Lafayette.

The Virgo Car

Malice has it that the Virgo husband is keener on his car than on his wife. This is nonsense of course, but it is true that Virgos are somewhat possessive of their cars, which they insist should be well constructed, modestly sized, and full of ingenious gadgets.

Broadly speaking the purpose of these gadgets is to save the Virgo money. Among them are a disembodied voice which snaps at you if you have forgotten to switch off the headlights, an alarm system which raises the entire neighbourhood if a stranger so much as touches your door, and a visual display unit full of sensible advice about the most economic speed at which to travel and when to check the oil and brakes. Virgos always use rev counters, again for economic reasons, and often tune their short-wave radios into the police. This is partly because they are afraid of being stopped but more because they like to keep themselves informed.

Virgos tend to fuss about their health and inside their ideal vehicle they would have a fruit-juice dispenser to spare them from the noxious beverages brewed in the name of tea or coffee at grub-ridden motorway service stations.

Practicality is the characteristic of the Virgo car. Its owner spends much time and even money installing devices designed to improve its performance and lower fuel consumption. He has a horror of rust and coats the bodywork in at least four layers of wax. Indeed he is obsessive about maintenance generally. Convinced that his car was last off the assembly-line on a Friday afternoon, he is forever anticipating ways in which it might go wrong.

In spite of their normally law-abiding nature, Virgos do tend to drink on long trips. Since nothing infuriates them more than to be breathalyzed just above the legal limit, their ideal car would feature a radar detector in order to chart police movements.

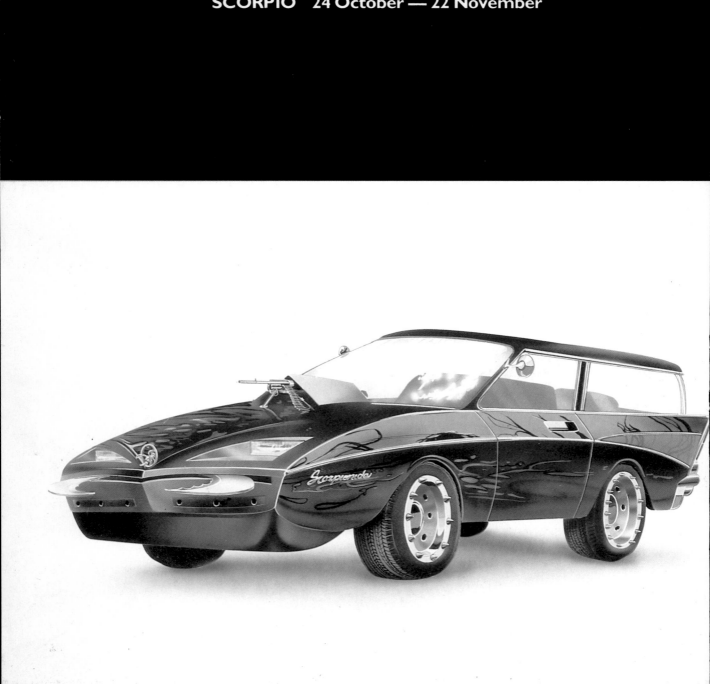

The Virgo's favourite colour is pale blue, although, like the Gemini, he also favours two-toned schemes. He is particularly fond of Japanese cars, whose manufacturers have a legendary eye for detail and share his lust for gadgets. This is not surprising, since Japan is an Aries country with a Virgo ascendant.

1 Hidden spare wheel
2 Four coats of wax
3 Video cameras
4 Radar detector
5 VDU
6 Rev counter
7 Fruit-juice dispenser
8 Burglar alarm
9 Short-wave radio
10 Fire extinguisher

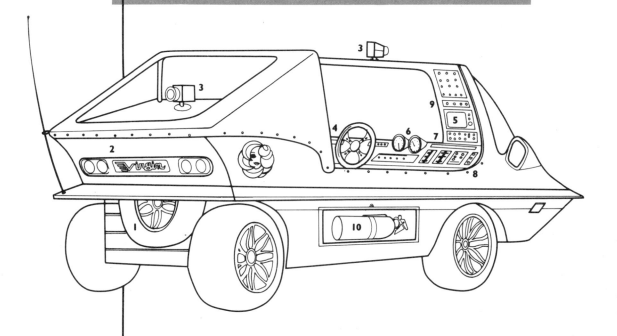

Fact or Fiction?

The characteristics given to Virgos are not particularly appealing. Insensitivity is a strong feature, but the role of comedian hardly fits real-life Virgos like James Hunt, the former World Champion, who could do with a sense of humour to cope with his fellow-television commentator, Murray Walker; Clay Regazzoni, who may have a comic streak but never reveals it; and Stirling Moss, a cocky man who thrusts his chin outward and upward as if to give him inches. The only time such Virgos are funny is when they are trying to be serious.

Cartier suggests that the Virgo husband prefers a car to a wife. Maybe so, but much depends on the number of spouses and how many times they have been traded in. Peter Sellers comes to mind. He was a truly comic Virgo who was enthusiastic about women and cars, but each girl was so delectable that no right-minded person could compare them to inanimate objects. The Virgo fascination with gadgets is certainly true of Moss, whose house has many novel innovations.

One thing is certain. No Virgo would own a car so hideously designed as the one described. Preference would go to the creations of Walter Owen Bentley, whose working life began as a railway workshop apprentice. He raced DFP cars, switched to piston, then turned to aero-engine design in the First World War. Bentley cars appeared between 1919 and 1931 from the works at Cricklewood. After Rolls-Royce bought the name, Bentley transferred his designing skills to Lagonda, producing the celebrated V12 engine and in 1950 the twin-cam six-cylinder for Aston Martin and Lagonda.

Cartier declares that Virgos are more cerebral than emotional. Regarding Bentley that was probably true, only in his case the end product was superbly designed. The marque of Bentley won the Le Mans Twenty-four-Hour Race five times: first in 1924, and in four successive years from 1927. In 1922 Walter Owen drove one of his own cars into fourth place in the TT in the Isle of Man – and Bentleys won the team prize.

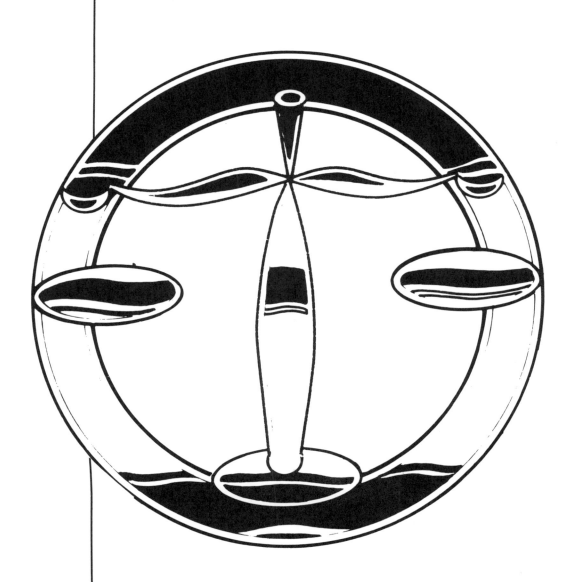

LIBRA
24 SEPTEMBER–23 OCTOBER

People often say that Librans are unstable. This is unfair. Courage, strength and a sharp nose for business are all Libran characteristics. Nevertheless, their temperament is highly artistic. They react to things in an extreme way, conceive fierce loyalties, and are inclined to be rather sentimental. Like Pisceans, they abhor ugliness, and never quite recover from the shock of finding that the world is full of it. For Librans, beauty is fundamental to peace. Many of them are impassioned idealists.

Since they cannot transform the world, Librans tend to settle for transforming their environment. Their aim is to make it as beautiful as possible. This is laudable in itself, but it can have unfortunate consequences. For example, Librans are rather fussy. They spend too much time on their appearance. They hate vulgarity, and are quick to criticize your taste. Many are hypochondriacs, making a great nuisance of themselves with relentless lists of imaginary ailments. At their worst they are aggressive and misanthropic.

Love is life to the Libran. He cannot do without it. Unlike the Taurus, however, he is not much interested in family affection. Instead he idealizes sexual love. Married Librans are often so passionate about their partners that they regard their children as tiresome adjuncts. This causes much distress.

Librans make good salesmen, especially in luxury trades such as fashion and design. At their best they are witty, attractive and full of charm. They are also uncannily intuitive. One hesitates to say that they have a sixth sense, but it is a fact that they can often predict people's fortunes and many of them dabble in the supernatural. They are sociable by nature, but do not like crowds.

Physique
Tall and slim. Fine features, russet or brown hair, remarkably warm voice.

Planetary Influences
Venus and Saturn. Venus characterizes love, in this case erotic love, and Saturn represents courage, and a tendency to pessimism.

Famous Librans
Modern figures: Mahatma Ghandi, General Eisenhower, David Ben-Gurion, Brigitte Bardot, John Lennon.
Historical figures: William Penn (Founder of Pennsylvania).

The Libran Car

Vacuum cleaners, waste-disposal units and modern cars are alike abhorrent to the Libran. He is hopelessly nostalgic and yearns for the days when driving had a sense of style. In the twenties he would have owned a Cord, a Hudson or an Isotta Fraschini. None of these cars can be found today except in museums, or rotting in neglected scrap-yards.

To construct the Libran's ideal car you have to go back to the days before romance succumbed to plastic – to 1929, to be exact. It has spoked wheels with tyres rimmed in white, a tool-box attached to the running-board, and an elegant trunk fastened to the back with leather straps. A spare wheel adorns each of the two front mudguards.

Luxury and sensual pleasures abound inside. The cushions are pink and velvet, the seatbelts are embroidered in silk, and on top of the teak-lined bar is a blue Ming vase containing a single Papa-Meilland rose. The bar itself sports Baccarat crystal goblets studded in diamonds. A Wedgwood tea-set sits precariously on the coffee-table and, amid the distinctive smell of octane petrol (which is nowadays unobtainable), one gets a whiff of Yardley's lavender.

This is fantasy of course. Nevertheless it is a fact that Librans are besotted with vintage cars. Many buy imitation models, such as the famous Excalibur, or one of the variety of classic cars manufactured in California. Poorer Librans buy ancient Fords and revamp them themselves.

The Libran pampers his car as you might pamper your baby. For instance, he will never let your baby inside it for fear of spoiling the interior. His favourite colour is lilac or pink.

1 Spoked wheels with white-rimmed tyres
2 Spare wheel mounted on mudguard
3 Copper headlights
4 Ornate nineteenth-century clock
5 Wedgwood tea-set
6 Bar with Baccarat crystal goblets
7 Ming vase
8 Leather-strapped trunk

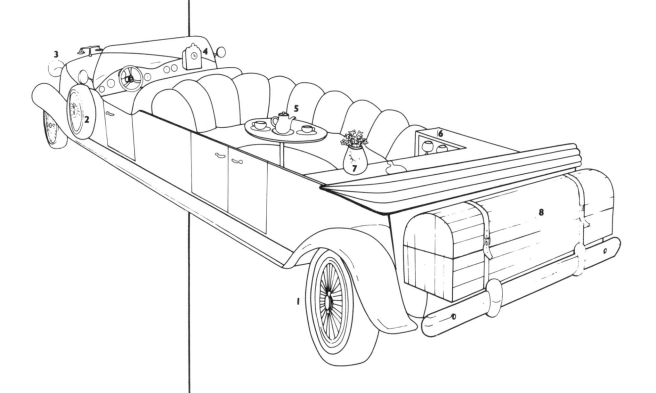

Fact or Fiction?

The best counter to Cartier's altogether fanciful description of the Libran and his car is the story of a man of yeoman stock who began as an apprentice to a bicycle repairer in Oxford. He was the eldest of seven children, but only one sister survived with him beyond infancy. His father, a draper's assistant, set him up in his own bicycle business when he was sixteen, with a capital of £4. So began the career of William Richard Morris, later to become Viscount Nuffield, industrialist and philanthropist, who during his lifetime was able to donate some £30 million to causes for the alleviation of human suffering. It all came from the Morris cars, the first being produced in 1913. He never claimed to be a designer, but a businessman who gave good value for money. The sales figures speak for themselves. In 1951 the two millionth Morris car came off the assembly line. He collected many famous companies into his corporate net, and in 1952 merged Nuffield with Austin to form BMC. That gives some idea of what a single-minded Libran can achieve.

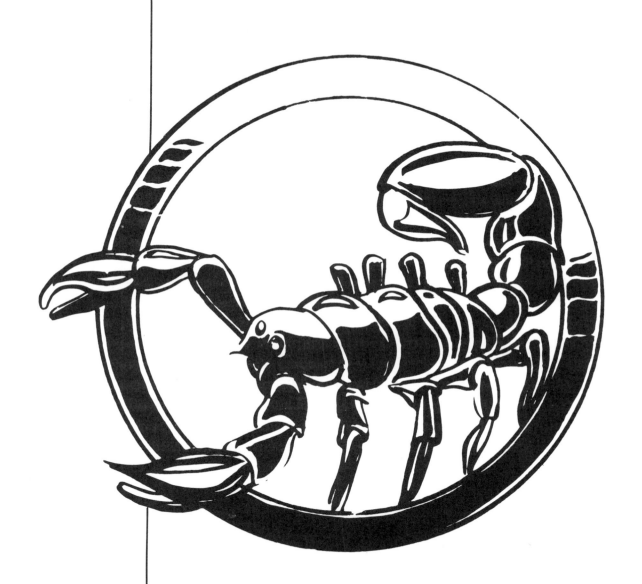

SCORPIO
24 OCTOBER–22 NOVEMBER

Death intrigues the Scorpio. He will spend hours mulling over its terrors. He exults in the thrill of danger and the horrors of the dark. Moreover, because he is so accustomed to such things he loses his fear of them. He is consequently very heroic. If a house is burning to the ground the last person to abandon it will be a Scorpio.

Sadly, the Scorpio's obsession with mystery and the Occult can lead him from the path of virtue. Although he excels in innocent pursuits such as tennis he is equally prepared to succeed dishonestly, and loves nothing better than a shady business deal. He is fiercely independent and knows exactly what he wants, but he is without much scruple as to how he might get it. He dominates in everything he does.

Losing is one of the few things the Scorpio is bad at. He regards it as a malevolent act of fate. If you succeed at a Scorpio's expense he will bear you a bitter grudge. He might even invoke the Satanic powers and cast a spell on you.

Scorpios make highly demanding parents. They are always telling their children that life is very tough. They expect their children to respond by becoming equally tough themselves.

Passion, whether in love or in defence of a belief or cause, has long been recognized as a Scorpion characteristic. They are excessively critical of other people but do not like other people to criticize them. This is a major fault but, to be fair, Scorpios usually struggle against it. They adore horror films and often subscribe to secret organizations, such as the Masons. Some of them are said to be sado-masochistic.

The female Scorpios are extremely bewitching. They tend to rebel against their environment, and many are ardent feminists. In matters of love they are as passionate as their male counterparts.

Scorpios insist on having the last word in arguments, and if you wish to retain their friendship, it is best to let them have it.

Physique
Average height, lithely limbed, proud features, usually dark complexion and hair.

Planetary Influences
Pluto and Mars. Mars symbolizes enthusiasm, courage and aggression. Pluto reigns over the twilight kingdom.

Famous Scorpios
Modern figures: Marie Curie, Leon Trotsky, General de Gaulle, Pablo Picasso, Richard Burton.
Historical figures: Marie-Antoinette.

The Scorpio Car

The Scorpio's ideal car is of angry appearance with great grinders jutting like claws from the front bumper and a machine-gun perched on the bonnet. Clad in sombre red-and-black armour-plated body panels, it cruises at 200mph with all the evil grace of a vampire. Its wheels are studded with little spikes reminiscent of Boadicea's chariots. At the push of a button on the demonic dashboard the vehicle self-destructs.

In lieu of such a monstrous model the Scorpio often settles for a Cadillac hearse. Purged of their formalin disinfectant and commemorative flowers, these vehicles make excellent campers. On foul nights, when the wind howls like a hyena and massy ravens encircle the doom-laden sky, you will often find the Scorpio parked in his hearse on a cliff-top overlooking the sea. Strains of Black Sabbath pour from the graphic equalizer. In the morning he returns to the drab routine of life with every appearance of being thoroughly refreshed.

Female Scorpios favour small Satanic sports cars, again in red and black, with cushions of bloody velvet and windows tinted green. Bold is the man who accepts a lift in such a vehicle. Being driven by a Scorpio is like being ferried by Charon into the Underworld, only it happens much faster. Remember, the road is the Scorpio's favourite arena for his favourite pastime — duelling with death.

1 Flame-throwers
2 Grinders
3 Phosphorous headlamps
4 Machine-gun
5 Graphic equalizer playing Black Sabbath
6 Shroud-draped seats
7 Self-destructing explosives chamber
8 Spiked hubcaps

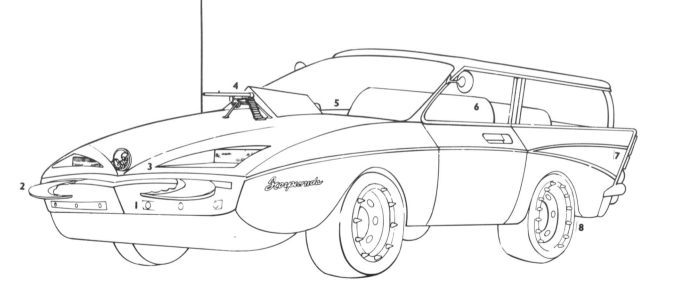

Fact or Fiction?

Scorpios ought to be easily recognizable when on parole by courtesy of Lord Longford. Cartier says they are preoccupied with death and the Occult and enjoy watching horror films, which in understandable as they tend to be sado-masochistic. The vehicle Cartier pictures as ideal for such creeps is a modified hearse.

Not many would wish to be identified with such zodiac-influenced oddities. To introduce a note of sanity I recall a Scorpio who contributed richly to his fellow-men with donations of millions of pounds, particularly to hospitals. That man was Herbert Austin, a farmer's son who went to Australia with an uncle in 1884 and became an engineering apprentice at Langlands Foundry, Melbourne. Later he moved to the Wolseley Sheep Shearing Machine Company where he became manager. He returned to England in 1893 and continued to work for the Wolseley Company as Production Manager in their Birmingham workshops. The firm made bicycle and machine parts as well as its main product. With growing experience Austin took out a number of patents for his own inventions and in 1911 he became Chairman of the company. He had always been interested in the possibilities of motor vehicles and had produced his first Wolseley car, a three-wheeler, in 1895. In 1922 he introduced the 'Baby Austin', a seven-horse-power car which for the first time brought motoring within reach of those with modest incomes. Whether credit for his remarkable success was due to the influence of Scorpio is a moot point. What is certain is that the breakthrough stemmed from the novelty and efficiency of his designs. He was a skilled engineer who graduated by force of energy, originality and determination from the workshop floor to management of a vast business.

SAGITTARIUS
23 NOVEMBER–21 DECEMBER

SAGITTARIUS
23 NOVEMBER–21 DECEMBER

Like Librans, Sagittarians have a strong sense of intuition, which they use to their own advantage. Indeed, they seem to rely upon it far more than upon any conventional mode of judgement. They can see trouble brewing a mile off and seldom get into awkward situations. Their uncanny knack of knowing what you are thinking enables them to predict what you are going to say. As a result they are brilliant at arguing. Often they seem to bring you round to their point of view without your being aware of it. Not surprisingly, many of them are salesmen and politicians.

The Sagittarian boss (of which there are many) is the sort of person who borrows all your ideas and leaves you with the impression that they were his all along.

Sagittarians love wide-open spaces and the various sports associated with them, such as hunting or shooting. Their aim is very direct, whether tilted against some hapless pigeon or at a coveted ambition. This directness has its merits – for example, Sagittarians never dissemble – but it often upsets people. Nevertheless, it is generally better to say what you think instead of what other people want to hear, and in this respect Sagittarians are very honest. They are also loyal and determined.

If you hope to win the affections of a female Sagittarian do not under any circumstances show off in front of her or shower her with empty compliments. This she cannot abide. Male Sagittarians are similarly opposed to flattery. They are extraordinarily down-to-earth in romantic affairs, secure in the knowledge that to be successful they simply have to be themselves.

Sagittarians are active creatures and dislike being confined, but they are good at making the best use of whatever space is available to them. They adore taking risks. Many of them gamble at poker or bridge, and although the wiser Sagittarians try to curb their passion for this vice, others resort to crime in order to finance it.

Physique
Above average height, extremely gesticulative, impressive features, high forehead and prominent nose.

Planetary Influence
Jupiter — symbolizes business sense, science and philosophy.

Famous Sagittarians
Modern figures: Winston Churchill, Charlton Heston, Jane Fonda, Maria Callas, Frank Sinatra, Patrick McGowan.
Historical figures: Beethoven, Berlioz.

The Sagittarian Car

When it comes to cars, Sagittarians think on a grand scale. Not for them the diminutive hatchbacks with their niggardly fuel consumption and Toytown appearance. The Mercedes 600, a six-windowed Cadillac or even a La Brink truck are more to their taste.

It is an extraordinary fact that the majority of big-time gangsters were Sagittarians. This is not to say that all Sagittarians are thugs. Nevertheless they do tend to identify with the specious glamour of organized crime and this is reflected in their choice of ideal car.

Solidity and power are the chief characteristics of this vehicle. Its windows are tinted and bullet-proof, and only the driver knows how to operate its ingenious central locking system. Mounted on revolving drums at each end of the car is a variety of number plates which the chauffeur switches from time to time in order to bamboozle potential pursuers. The reinforced bodywork is punctuated with hidden alcoves from which machine-guns emerge at the press of a button, and at the back a curious gadget which pours nails on to the road may be similarly activated. Sirens and flashing lights adorn the roof. A feature of the exhaust pipe discourages other drivers from getting too close by showering their windscreens with used oil. The colour of the car is deepest burgundy.

The Sagittarian is a natural boss and he likes his car to convey this fact. Even within the constraints of reality he will opt for a large, solid-looking vehicle. Nobody offered stouter resistance to the craze for economy-conscious Toyotas. In Toronto a garage-owner specializes in renovating old limousines re-nowned for their inordinate consumption of fuel. Against every prediction he makes a vast amount of money from this enterprise. Deprived of his Sagittarian customers, he would barely break even.

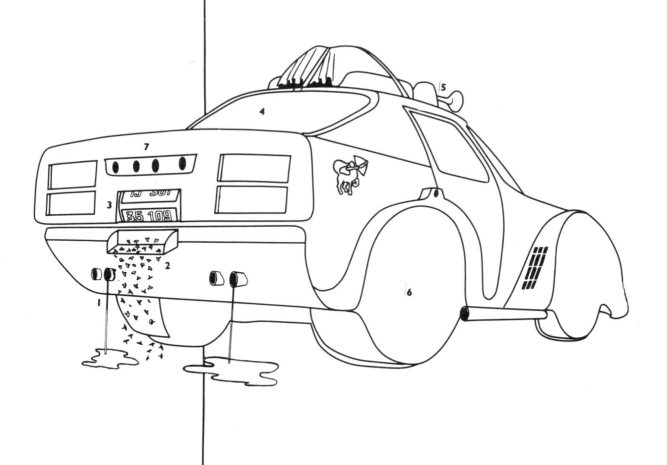

1 Oil-emitting exhaust system
2 Nail dispenser
3 Revolving number plates
4 Bullet-proof windows
5 Flashing light and siren
6 Armour-plated tyres
7 Hidden machine-guns

Fact or Fiction?

I counter Cartier's ideal Sagittarian car with the story of a citizen of the Ottoman empire. Alec Issigonis, born in Smyrna in 1906, came to this country with his mother in 1922. Penniless, any prospects of being a success in life depended on sweat and talent. Battersea Polytechnic was the start, but he failed in exams. The industrial Midlands was the answer; first Humber, then Morris Motors, where he developed their first independent front suspension before producing the post-war Morris Minor. His progress continued with three years at Alvis, then to BMC at Longbridge, where his ingenuity as a designer resulted in the sensational Mini. As the corporation's technical director, Alec introduced many brilliant innovations, not least being the transverse-engine front-drive layout of the Mini, which somehow leaves the Cartier brain-child with its revolving number plates, bullet-proof windows, armour-plated tyres and nail dispenser a likely candidate for post-Borstal joy rides.

CAPRICORN
22 DECEMBER–20 JANUARY

People who are born under the sign of Capricorn are practical and conservative. They like to be in control of things. Speculative thinking does not interest them, unless they can perceive some useful purpose in it. Nor are they much interested in art.

The Capricorn is generally self-confident. He is inclined to be right-wing in politics. His primary concern is to achieve success, which he measures in material terms. Within the hierarchical structure of most offices the Capricorn is eager to worm his way to the top, and he will not hesitate to curry favour with important people who might help him. In this manner he often becomes a pillar of the establishment, such as a politician or prominent businessman.

Curiously, once the Capricorn has reached the top of his particular ladder, he does not crow about it, unlike his Leo and Sagittarian counterparts. Aware of the unpredictability of fortune and of the volatile nature of economic forces, he tends to live well below his means. He is not flamboyant and, in his anxiety to elude the attention of envious contemporaries or the Inland Revenue, he is happy to sink into bourgeois anonymity. Indeed, he is sometimes rather miserly.

Capricorns have a fierce sense of principle and will do all they can to instil it in their children. Dominated by Saturn, they are not by nature prone to fun. They will try to appear sociable, but this is only because they think it is expected of them. Secretly, most Capricorns regard the prospect of a wild night out with horror. They much prefer sedate domestic evenings, with perhaps a select group of friends. They have a very strong sense of the importance of the family, which their children can find insular and oppressive.

Imagination is not a Capricorn characteristic. Consequently if they get themselves into an awkward situation they are often at a loss as to how to get out of it. This is perhaps their biggest failing. The weaker Capricorns get deeply depressed if their lives are not progressing according to plan, and this can lead to drink or drugs.

Fortunately, such cases are rare. Most Capricorns climb steadily to the top of the tree. They are full of industry and determination, but when they do encounter failure they are not at all good at shrugging it off, and often bear grudges.

Physique
Slender, quick and precise movements, leaden complexion, long and slender face.

Planetary Influence
Saturn — characterized by perseverance, courage, inflexibility, and a tendency to pessimism.

Famous Scorpios
Modern figures: Stalin, Pablo Casals, Humphrey Bogart, Richard Nixon, Martin Luther King, Mohammed Ali.
Historical figures: Isaac Newton, Benjamin Franklin, Edgar Allan Poe.

The Capricorn Car

Like the Libran, the Capricorn will spend neither time nor effort in choosing his car. If his own model is several years out of date, which is likely to be the case, he will be blithely unaware of it. His neighbours may suffer penury in order to afford the flashiest car on the market, but the Capricorn will opt for a vehicle which gained a certain reputation for reliability some ten or twenty years ago.

The Capricorn will tell you that the best way to wash your car is to leave it in the rain. Maintenance holds no interest for him. Car-lovers scoff at his easy indifference to power-assisted steering and electronic fuel injection, but seldom can they rival his substantial house, his handsome job and the steady sense of purpose which illuminates his life.

In Europe, the Capricorn boss is likely to roll up to work in a beat-up Peugeot 404. This is partly to persuade employees of his modesty, and also to give the impression that he is ploughing his profits back into the company. But he is not above hiding a superior vehicle in his garage at home. His American counterpart cruises around in a rusty seventies Chevrolet.

One of the reasons why so many Capricorns become politicians is that the state provides them with transport, thereby relieving them of the irksome responsibility of car-ownership. Nothing you can say will persuade them that driving is enjoyable, and their attitude towards the motor industry is positively snobbish. Woe betide the car salesman who encounters a Capricorn customer. Eager salestalk will be met with stony contempt.

This is not to say that the Capricorn never owns a good car. If he is convinced that such a vehicle will last longer and cause less trouble, he will pay a lot of money for it. But he will never own a flashy car. For colours he favours the dullest browns and charcoal greys. It is almost as if he chooses his car with the express purpose of discouraging people from taking an interest in him. Certainly it is most unlikely to excite any romantic attraction, but then, Capricorns are rarely romantics.

1 Bumper held together with string
2 Torches in lieu of defective headlamps
3 Sponge tied to the end of windscreen wiper
4 Improvised sunroof
5 Jammed door
6 Children's initials drawn in dust
7 Poorly balanced wheels

Fact or Fiction?

Capricorn I have left to the last because its zodiac influences should have affected my life. Naturally when I read Cartier's comments I find myself in agreement with the flattering bits. I do like to be in control of things. I am self-confident. I do measure success in material terms. On the other hand I do not worm my way to the top or curry favour; the opposite would be nearer the mark. I am not flamboyant, but I have never courted bourgeois anonymity. It is true that I enjoy the company of a select group of friends, but I do not shun awkward situations and never get depressed to the point where drink or drugs are necessary. I complete my halo by agreeing that I am industrious and determined, but do not bear grudges.

When it comes to the special Capricorn car, I find myself in complete disagreement. No one in their senses would be seen in such a derelict vehicle. I rest my case on some of the commercial projects in which I was involved at BRM. We designed, developed and tested a single-overhead-camshaft version of the Reliant 850cc engine, based on the existing unit and formulated to give an output of 55-60bhp with torque characteristics suitable for normal road use. We had a long-standing partnership with Chrysler for the production of a BRM-engined Avenger, powered by 125-135bhp BRM-tuned twin-cam sixteen-valve engines which retained the 1600cc inline